What if life were perfect?

What if you lived in a perfect world of perfect people and perfect possessions, with everyone and everything doing the perfect thing at the perfect time?

What if you had everything you wanted, and only what you wanted, exactly as you wanted, precisely when you wanted it?

What if, after a perfect length of time, you decided, "Perfection is a perfect bore."

What if, at that point in your perfect world, you created a button marked, "Surprise."

What if you walked over, considered all that might be contained in the concept of "surprise," decided, "Anything's better than perfect boredom," took a deep breath, pushed the button . . .

. . . and found yourself where you are right now—feeling what you're feeling now, thinking what you're thinking now, with everything in your life precisely the way it is now—reading this book.

Books by Peter McWilliams

LOVE 101
To Love Oneself is the Beginning of a Lifelong Romance

You Can't Afford the Luxury of a Negative Thought:
A Book for People with Any Life-Threatening Illness—
Including Life

Focus on the Positive: The You Can't Afford the Luxury
of a Negative Thought Workbook

LIFE 101: Everything We Wish
We Had Learned About Life In School—But Didn't

DO IT! Let's Get Off Our Buts

The Portable DO IT!

All of the above titles are available on unabridged audio tapes.

The Portable

LIFE 101

179 essential lessons from the *New York Times* bestseller *LIFE 101: Everything We Wish We Had Learned in Life In School—But Didn't*

by Peter McWilliams

Prelude Press
8159 Santa Monica Boulevard
Los Angeles, CA 90046
1-800-LIFE-101
©1995 By Prelude Press, Inc. All rights reserved.
Cover and book design: Paul LeBus

Printed in the United States by Vaughan Printing

Introduction

By the time we graduate from high school, we have spent some 14,500 hours in the classroom. But in all that time, did we learn—or even explore—the meaning of life?

We learned how to calculate the square root of an isosceles triangle (invaluable in daily life), but did we learn how to forgive ourselves and others?

We dissected a frog, but perhaps never explored the dynamics of human relationships.

We know what pi is, but we're not sure who we are.

We may know how to diagram a sentence, but we may not know how to love ourselves.

Did we learn about worthiness (and how to get it), the power of thoughts (and how to use them), or the value of mistakes?

Did anyone teach us how to use guilt, resentment, pain and fear for our upliftment, learning, and growth?

Did we learn our purpose in life?

These were some of the questions I set out to answer when I wrote *LIFE 101: Everything We Wish We Had Learned About Life In School—But Didn't*. I wanted it to be a practical, useful, sometimes funny gathering of techniques, methods, and ideas that worked for me. It was published in 1990.

Some of the people who read *LIFE 101* asked for a condensed version—the essential lessons presented in a more portable format. Sort of the Cliffs Notes to life.

Hence, *The Portable LIFE 101.*

To enjoy *The Portable LIFE 101,* there's no need to read the original *LIFE 101.* (If this is the portable version, what should I call the other *LIFE 101?* The stationary version? The immovable edition? *LIFE 101 Classic?* What do you think?)

For some, *The Portable LIFE 101* will be a review. For others, a preview.

And what are my credentials for teaching about life? Well, I am an honored graduate of the School of Hard Knocks. From there I went on to the University of Adversity (an institution in which I am still enrolled).

I am, in fact, not a teacher but a fellow student in the school of life. I wrote *The Portable LIFE 101* mostly for myself. If you want to look over my shoulder as I remind myself of some of life's essential lessons, you are more than welcome.

So, welcome to *The Portable LIFE 101*.

School is in session!

— *Peter McWilliams*

The Portable
LIFE 101

–1–

That our educational system is not designed to teach us the "secrets of life" is no secret. In school, we learn how to do everything—except how to live.

★ ★ ★

At college age, you can tell
who is best at taking tests and going to school,
but you can't tell who the best people are.
That worries the hell out of me.

— BARNABY C. KEENEY

–2–

We know who wrote, "To be or not to be, that is the question," but we don't know the answer.

★　★　★

The essence of our effort
to see that every child has a chance
must be to assure each an equal opportunity,
not to become equal, but to become different—
to realize whatever unique potential of body,
mind and spirit he or she possesses.

— JOHN FISCHER

—3—

It seems that somewhere around eighteen (give or take ten years), something in us decides, "That's it, I've had it, I'm done. I know all I need to know. I'm not learning any more."

★ ★ ★

Life was meant to be lived
and curiosity must be kept alive.
One must never, for whatever reason,
turn his back on life.

— ELEANOR ROOSEVELT

– 4 –

"Commencement" does not just mean graduation; it means a new beginning.

★　★　★

Wear your learning,
like your watch,
in a private pocket:
and do not pull it out and strike it,
merely to show that you have one.

— EARL OF CHESTERFIELD
1774

—5—

Unraveling life's "mysteries" and discovering life's "secrets" (which are, in fact, neither mysterious nor secretive) may take the courage and determination found only in a self-motivated pursuit.

★ ★ ★

Only the curious will learn and
only the resolute overcome
the obstacles to learning.
The quest quotient has always excited
me more than the intelligence quotient.

— EUGENE S. WILSON

−6−

Life is for doing.

★ ★ ★

Things won are done;
joy's soul lies in the doing.

— SHAKESPEARE

−7−

One of the greatest—and simplest—tools for learning more and growing more is doing more.

★ ★ ★

Look, I really don't want to wax philosophic,
but I will say that if you're alive,
you got to flap your arms and legs,
you got to jump around a lot,
you got to make a lot of noise,
because life is the very opposite of death.

— MEL BROOKS

–8–

Life is for learning.

★   ★   ★

What a wonderful day we've had.
You have learned something,
and I have learned something.
Too bad we didn't learn it sooner.
We could have gone to the movies instead.

— BALKI BARTOKOMOUS
PERFECT STRANGERS

–9–

Life is for learning? Learning what?
You name it. There's a lot to learn.

★ ★ ★

Learning is not attained by chance,
it must be sought for with ardor
and attended to with diligence.

— ABIGAIL ADAMS
1780

–10–

Some of what we learned early on turned out to be true (the earth is round; if you want a friend, be a friend; cleanliness is next to impossible) and some of it turned out to be false (Santa Claus; the Tooth Fairy; Kansas is more fun than Oz).

★ ★ ★

Life is far too important a thing
ever to talk about.

— OSCAR WILDE

–11–

When life seems truly excremental, we can moan and groan, or we can—even in the midst of anger, terror, confusion, and pain—tell ourselves, "There must be a lesson in here someplace!"

★ ★ ★

Seek not, my soul, the life of the immortals;
but enjoy to the full the resources
that are within thy reach.

— PINDAR
438 B.C.

–12–

The good news is that we learn all we need to know—eventually.

★ ★ ★

*Good people are good
because they've come to
wisdom through failure.*
— WILLIAM SAROYAN

–13–

The more we learn, the more we do. The more we do, the more we learn. But in all this doing and learning, let's not forget one of the most important lessons of all—enjoyment.

★ ★ ★

How good is man's life, the mere living!
How fit to employ all the heart
and the soul and the senses
forever in joy!

— ROBERT BROWNING
1855

–14–

Life is for enjoying.

★ ★ ★

*I was thrown out of college
for cheating
on the metaphysics exam;
I looked into the soul
of the boy next to me.*

—WOODY ALLEN

–15–

Learn to enjoy the process of learning.

*   *   *

I didn't fail 1,000 times.
The light bulb was an invention
with 1,001 steps.

— EDISON

–16–

The best that life can do is *present* lessons to you. The learning is up to you.

★ ★ ★

With an eye made quiet
by the power of harmony,
and the deep power of joy,
we see into the life of things.

— WORDSWORTH

–17–

Life is a classroom.

★ ★ ★

Universities should be safe havens
where ruthless examination
of realities will not be distorted
by the aim to please
or inhibited
by the risk of displeasure.

—KINGMAN BREWSTER

–18–

It should come as no surprise that, if I think life is for learning, I would view the process of life itself as a classroom. But it's not a dull, sit-in-neat-little-rows-and-listen-to-some-puffed-up-professor-drone-on-and-on classroom. Life is (as I'm sure you've noticed) *experiential*. In that sense, life's more of a workshop.

★ ★ ★

Imagination is
more important than knowledge.

—ALBERT EINSTEIN

–19–

I like to think the workshop/classroom of life is perfectly arranged so that we learn what we need to learn, when we need to learn it, just the way we need to learn it.

★ ★ ★

Life is playing a violin solo in public
and learning the instrument
as one goes on.

— SAMUEL BUTLER

–20–

The classroom of life is not third grade, where all you will learn each day is neatly planned—including recess. What we *choose* to learn is fundamental to what we learn.

★ ★ ★

A life is a single letter
in the alphabet.
It can be meaningless.
Or it can be part of a great meaning.
— JEWISH THEOLOGICAL SEMINARY

–21–

Experience, it is said, is the best teacher—providing, of course, we become the best students.

★ ★ ★

The most important function of education
at any level is to develop
the personality of the individual
and the significance of his life
to himself and to others.

— GRAYSON KIRK

–22–

The *real* teacher of life is *you*. *You're* the one who must decide, of all that comes your way, what is true and what is not, what applies to you and what does not, what you learn now and what you *promise yourself* you'll learn later.

★ ★ ★

We learn simply by the exposure of living.
Much that passes for education
is not education at all but ritual.
The fact is that we are being educated
when we know it least.

— DAVID P. GARDNER

–23–

Who are you?

★ ★ ★

*Nobody can be
exactly like me.
Sometimes even I
have trouble doing it.*
— TALLULAH BANKHEAD

– 24 –

The discovery of that "You" is entirely your own—although the entire world is willing to help.

★ ★ ★

It's an unanswered question,
but let us still believe in the dignity
and importance of the question.
— TENNESSEE WILLIAMS

–25–

It doesn't take much inner listening to know that "in there" are many voices: speaking, singing, shouting, and whispering.

★ ★ ★

What the inner voice says
Will not disappoint the hoping soul.
— SCHILLER
1797

–26–

These voices have information—all of it useful. Some you can use by acting on; some you can use by doing precisely the opposite. It's a matter of knowing whether or not a given voice is on your side.

★ ★ ★

I thank you
for your voices, thank you,
Your most sweet voices.

— SHAKESPEARE

–27–

I'm going to take a clear, unequivocal, unambiguous position on God, religion, reincarnation, atheism, agnosticism and all that. My clear, unambiguous, and unequivocal position is this: I am clearly, unambiguously, unequivocally *not* taking a position.

★ ★ ★

*I have found the best way
to give advice to your children
is to find out what they want
and then advise them to do it.*

— HARRY S. TRUMAN

–28–

It's not that I don't *have* a point of view about each of these; it's just that the information in *LIFE 101* works regardless of my or your or *anyone's* point of view. There are certain forces—like the pull of gravity, the need for breathing, the desire for Häagen Dazs—that affect all of us regardless of beliefs. *LIFE 101* concerns itself with those "belief-proof" issues.

★ ★ ★

The most incomprehensible thing
about the world is that it is comprehensible.

— ALBERT EINSTEIN

–29–

I'd like to introduce a portion of life I call The Gap. The Gap is the area into which I put the many (often conflicting) beliefs people have about What's The Big Force Behind It All And How Does This Big Force Interact With Human Beings?

★ ★ ★

Jean-Paul Sartre *(arriving in heaven):*
It's not what I expected.

God: *What did you expect?*

Sartre: *Nothing.*

— *SCTV*

–30–

What *I* believe in is giving people the freedom to believe whatever they choose to believe.

★ ★ ★

I love God,
and when you get to know Him,
you find He's a Livin' Doll.

— JANE RUSSELL

–31–

Personally, I think we're all "old enough" to set aside the source, history, and trappings of certain techniques and ask of them a simple question: Do they work? (Do they produce the desired result? Do they get you what you want and need?)

★ ★ ★

My religion consists of a humble admiration
of the illimitable superior spirit
who reveals himself in the slight details
we are able to perceive
with our frail and feeble mind.

— ALBERT EINSTEIN

–32–

If it works for you, fine—use it; it's yours. If it doesn't work for you, let it go and try other things that may.

★ ★ ★

We don't receive wisdom;
we must discover it for ourselves
after a journey
that no one can take for us
or spare us.

— MARCEL PROUST

–33–

There is more going on than our senses perceive.

★ ★ ★

Sooner or later every one of us breathes
an atom that has been breathed before
by anyone you can think of
who has lived before us—
Michelangelo or George Washington
or Moses.

— JACOB BRONOWSKI

–34–

Unfortunately, our senses are limited; therefore our view of the world is limited.

★ ★ ★

*The important thing is science
is not so much to obtain new facts
as to discover new ways of thinking about them.*
— SIR WILLIAM BRAGG

–35–

There is more empty space in the book you're holding, than book. The atoms of the book give the *illusion* of solid ink on solid paper. They're not. It's just an illusion. If the electricity in the electron clouds were switched off, even for an instant, this book would crumble into atomic dust—an amount of dust not even visible to the naked eye. This book would appear to disappear. Poof.

★ ★ ★

In atomic physics, we can never speak of nature without, at the same time, speaking of ourselves.

— FRITJOF CAPRA

–36–

An atom (and thus all matter) is mostly empty space.
— ENCYCLOPÆDIA BRITANNICA

★ ★ ★

- Contrary to our perception and belief, there is more nothing than something, even in things that *appear* to have more something than nothing.

- Everything is always in motion, even things that don't appear to have moved in millions of years.

- The perception that things are solid and stationary is an illusion.

–37–

Life, it turns out, is not a struggle; it's a wiggle.

★ ★ ★

Any sufficiently advanced technology is indistinguishable from magic.

— ARTHUR C. CLARKE

–38–

When a child's primary memory of the communication from his or her parents ("the gods") is "no, don't, stop that, shouldn't, mustn't, shame, bad, bad, bad," what's the child being taught? That he or she can do no good; must be alert for failure at every moment, and *still* will fail; is a disappointment, a letdown, a failure. In short, a child begins to believe that he or she is fundamentally not good enough, destined for failure. In a word, *unworthy*.

★ ★ ★

The only reason I always try to meet and know the parents better is because it helps me to forgive their children.

— LOUIS JOHANNOT

–39–

If you think you're fooling people with your act of goodness, and you think you aren't all that good, maybe the one you're fooling is yourself.

★ ★ ★

The only good is knowledge and the only evil is ignorance.

— SOCRATES

–40–

Rule #1: Don't hurt yourself and don't hurt others.

★　★　★

The ideas I stand for are not mine.
I borrowed them from Socrates.
I swiped them from Chesterfield.
I stole them from Jesus.
And I put them in a book.
If you don't like their rules,
whose would you use?

— DALE CARNEGIE

–41–

Rule #2: Take care of yourself so you can help take care of others.

★ ★ ★

Exit according to rule,
first leg and then head.
Remove high heels and
synthetic stockings before evacuation:
Open the door, take out the recovery line
and throw it away.

— RUMANIAN NATIONAL AIRLINES
EMERGENCY INSTRUCTIONS

–42–

Rule #3: Use everything for your upliftment, learning, and growth.

★ ★ ★

*Is forbidden to steal towels, please.
If you are not person to do such
is please not to read notice.*

— SIGN IN TOKYO HOTEL

−43−

*If you're taking an essay exam on geography, and
the exam could be on any of the countries in the world,
study <u>one</u> country, and know it well.
Let's say you choose China.
When it comes time for the exam,
and the question is, "Write 1,000 words on Nigeria,"
you begin your essay, "Nigeria is nothing like China . . ."
and proceed to write everything you know about China.*

— QUENTIN CRISP

★ ★ ★

Is that cheating? No. That's life. That's using everything for your learning, upliftment, and growth.

–44–

*Experimentation
is an active science.*
— CLAUDE BERNARD

★ ★ ★

Experiment. Make your life
an active science.

–45–

As far as I can tell, the only thing you can take charge of is *the space within your skin*. That's it. Everything (and, especially, everyone) else does not belong to what you can take charge of.

★ ★ ★

The last of the human freedoms—
to choose one's attitude
in any given set of circumstances,
to choose one's own way.

— VIKTOR FRANKL

–46–

To the degree we do not have charge of our minds, bodies and emotions, we have our work cut out for us. Do we really have any *extra* time to spend taking charge of *others?*

★　★　★

To be one's self and unafraid
whether right or wrong,
is more admirable than
the easy cowardice of
surrender to conformity.

— IRVING WALLACE

–47–

To observe, don't *do* anything; simply notice the inner process. The voices demanding you do this, move there, or scratch whatever may rise to screaming crescendo. Don't do anything; continue to observe.

★ ★ ★

You do not need to leave your room.
Remain sitting at your table and listen.
Do not even listen, simply wait.
Do not even wait, be quite still and solitary.
The world will freely offer itself to you
to be unmasked, it has no choice,
it will roll in ecstasy at your feet.

— FRANZ KAFKA

–48–

What is that inner demand? What is the voice (or voices) that *insists* you do this, or run away from that? Why do you sometimes follow that voice automatically—maybe even unconsciously? The answers to these questions lie in observation.

★ ★ ★

If you resist evil,
as soon as it's gone, you'll fold.

— KEN KESEY

–49–

Open your mind.

★ ★ ★

*Faced with the choice
between changing one's mind and
proving there is no need to do so,
almost everyone
gets busy on the proof.*

— JOHN KENNETH GALBRAITH

–50–

Strengthen your body.

★ ★ ★

*You're obviously
suffering from
delusions of adequacy.*
— ALEXIS CARRINGTON
DYNASTY

–51–

Fortify your emotions.

★ ★ ★

If you do not wish to be prone to anger,
do not feed the habit;
give it nothing which may tend to its increase.
At first, keep quiet and count the days when
you were not angry: "I used to be angry
every day, then every other day: next,
every two, then every three days!"
and if you succeed in passing thirty days,
sacrifice to the gods in thanksgiving.

— EPICTETUS

–52–

Try new things.

★ ★ ★

Life is a series of inspired follies.
The difficulty is to find them to do.
Never lose a chance:
it doesn't come every day.

— GEORGE BERNARD SHAW

–53–

The underlying question in trying new things: Would I hurt myself *physically* (not emotionally, not mentally) if I did this? Not *could* (we *could* hurt ourselves doing almost anything), but *would*. If the answer is no, then do it.

★ ★ ★

What we have to do is to be forever
curiously testing new opinions
and courting new impressions.

— WALTER PATER
1873

–54–

Acceptance is such an important commodity, some have called it "the first law of personal growth." Acceptance is simply seeing something the way it is and saying, "That's the way it is."

★ ★ ★

And that's the way it is.
— WALTER CRONKITE

–55–

Acceptance is not approval, consent, permission, authorization, sanction, concurrence, agreement, compliance, sympathy, endorsement, confirmation, support, ratification, assistance, advocating, backing, maintaining, authenticating, reinforcing, cultivating, encouraging, furthering, promoting, aiding, abetting or even *liking* what is.

Acceptance is saying, "It is what it is, and what is is what is."

Philosophers from Gertrude Stein ("A rose is a rose is a rose") to Popeye ("I am what I am") have understood acceptance.

–56–

Until we truly accept *everything,* we can not see clearly. We will always be looking through the filters of "must's," "should's," "ought-to's," "have-to's," and prejudices.

★ ★ ★

Education is the ability
to listen to almost anything
without losing your temper
or your self-confidence.

— ROBERT FROST

–57–

When you're in a state of nonacceptance, it's difficult to learn. A clenched fist cannot receive a gift, and a clenched psyche—grasped tightly against the reality of what *must not be* accepted—cannot easily receive a lesson.

★ ★ ★

No matter how cynical you get,
it is impossible to keep up.

— LILY TOMLIN

–58–

Whatever we find "true" about the people and things around us, is also true about ourselves.

★ ★ ★

*When we see men
of a contrary character,
we should turn inwards
and examine ourselves.*

— CONFUCIUS

–59–

When we evaluate anything outside ourselves, what we are doing is looking into a mirror; the mirror reflects back to us information about ourselves.

★ ★ ★

I bid him look into the lives of men
as though into a mirror,
and from others to take an example for himself.

— TERENCE
159 B.C.

–60–

You may not always *like* what you see in the mirror; you may not always be comfortable with it; but, if you want to learn about yourself more quickly, looking at yourself in the mirror of people and things is a valuable tool.

★ ★ ★

*If you want to make
the world a better place,
take a look at yourself
and make a change.*

— MICHAEL JACKSON
"MAN IN THE MIRROR"

–61–

Relationships truly take place inside ourselves. We have a relationship with anyone or anything we encounter. What we do inside ourselves about the people (and things) we choose to be in relationship with can be one of the greatest learning tools we can use.

★   ★   ★

*The best mirror
is an old friend.*

— GEORGE HERBERT
1651

–62–

All that good advice you've been giving to others (or would gladly give them if they only had the intelligence to ask) finally has a home. You.

* * *

There is no human problem
which could not be solved
if people would simply
do as I advise.

—GORE VIDAL

–63–

When something happens to you, you can explore it and probably see that you had *something* to do with its taking place. You either created it, promoted it, or—at the very least—*allowed* it.

★ ★ ★

Crystal: *Do you realize that most people use two percent of their mind's potential?*

Roseanne: *That much, huh?*

— ROSEANNE

–64–

True accountability has three parts. First, acknowledge that you had *something* to do with what's happened. Second, explore your response options. Third, take a corrective action.

★ ★ ★

When you make a mistake,
admit it. If you don't,
you only make matters worse.

— WARD CLEAVER
LEAVE IT TO BEAVER

–65–

This is a lifetime of good-byes. In our time, we will say good-bye to cherished people, things, and ideas. Eventually, we say good-bye to life itself with our death. Learn to say a good good-bye.

★ ★ ★

When an emotional injury takes place,
the body begins a process as natural
as the healing of a physical wound.
Let the process happen.
Trust that nature will do the healing.
Know that the pain will pass and, when it passes,
you will be stronger, happier, more sensitive and aware.

— HOW TO SURVIVE
THE LOSS OF A LOVE

–66–

There are three distinct, yet overlapping, phases of recovery. We go through each phase no matter what the loss. The only difference is the duration and intensity of feeling. The first stage is *shock / denial / numbness.* The second stage is *fear / anger / depression.* The third stage is *understanding / acceptance / moving on.*

★ ★ ★

In the darkest hour the soul is replenished and given strength to continue and endure.

— HEART WARRIOR CHOSA

–67–

Contrary to popular belief, it's not *attachment* that causes loss—attachment feels fine. It's *de*tachment that hurts. Learn to let go.

★ ★ ★

I don't want the cheese,
I just want to get out of the trap.
— SPANISH PROVERB

–68–

Record each day, in some way: the lessons you learn, the good you do, the good that happens to you, the insights you have, and anything else that seems of importance or interest.

★ ★ ★

Keep a diary,
and someday your diary
will keep you.

— MAE WEST

–69–

What is *light*? Whatever that invisible force is that responds to human interaction, that's what we mean by light.

★ ★ ★

As we penetrate into matter,
nature does not show us
any isolated "basic building blocks,"
but rather appears as
a complicated web of relations
between the various parts of the whole.

— FRITJOF CAPRA

−70−

Using the light is very easy. You simply ask that the light (you can imagine it as a clear, pure white light) be sent somewhere for the highest good of all concerned. That's it. That's using the light.

* * *

I'm going to turn on the light,
and we'll be two people in a room
looking at each other and wondering
why on earth we were afraid of the dark.

— GALE WILHELM

–71–

How do we know the light "worked"? Sometimes the situation changes, sometimes our attitude about the situation changes, and sometimes both.

★ ★ ★

Man is his own star, and the soul that can
Render an honest and a perfect man
Commands all light, all influence, all fate.

— JOHN FLETCHER
1647

–72–

Things may not change the way we want them to change. The light is not a bellhop in the sky. It will not do what you want at the expense of others—or yourself. To have *all* of our desires fulfilled would be a curse.

★ ★ ★

When the gods
choose to punish us,
they merely answer our prayers.

— OSCAR WILDE

−73−

If you listen carefully, you'll hear (or sense) a voice inside yourself. It's the voice of your Master Teacher. (I'll use the word *voice,* but for you it may be an image or a feeling or a sensation or any combination of these.) It may not be the loudest voice "in there," but it's often the most consistent, patient, and persistent one. What does your inner teacher sound like? It's the one that just said, "I sound like this."

★ ★ ★

Always keep a window in the attic open;
not just cracked: open.

— HENRY JAMES

–74–

Your Master Teacher knows all you need to learn, the perfect timing for your learning it, and the ideal way of teaching it to you. You don't *create* a Master Teacher—that's already been done. You *discover* your Master Teacher.

★ ★ ★

If you have built castles in the air,
your work need not be lost;
that is where they should be.
Now put the foundations under them.

— THOREAU

–75–

Your Master Teacher is not the only Master Teacher in your life. Far from it. Master Teachers disguise themselves as some of the most potentially powerful learning tools in our lives: mistakes, guilt and resentment, fear, pain and disease, stubbornness, addictions, depression, death, emergencies—all the things most people would, if they could, eliminate.

★ ★ ★

A problem is a chance for you to do your best.
— DUKE ELLINGTON

–76–

Mistakes, obviously, show us what needs improving. Without mistakes, how would we know what we had to work on?

★ ★ ★

Mistakes are the portals of discovery.
— JAMES JOYCE

–77–

In Hollywood, mis-takes are common. ("That was wonderful, darlings. Now let's get ready for take two.") Give yourself as many re-takes as you need. Stars do it. Why not you?

★ ★ ★

Pick yourself up, dust yourself off,
start all over again.
— DOROTHY FIELDS

–78–

To avoid situations in which you *might* make mistakes may be the biggest mistake of all.

★ ★ ★

Aim for success, not perfection.
Never give up your right to be wrong,
because then you will lose the ability
to learn new things and move forward with your life.
Remember that fear always lurks behind perfectionism.
Confronting your fears and allowing yourself
the right to be human can, paradoxically,
make you a far happier and more productive person.

— DR. DAVID M. BURNS

–79–

Guilt is anger directed at ourselves—at what we did or did not do. Resentment is anger directed at others—at what they did or did not do.

★ ★ ★

Everything
that irritates us about others can lead us
to an understanding of ourselves.

— CARL JUNG

–80–

The cure for guilt and resentment? Forgiveness. The preventative? Acceptance. The best reason to do good? Loving. And if you forget any of this, the Master Teacher will be there, just before you veer off-course, asking gently, with that first tinge of guilt or resentment, "Would you rather be right or be happy?" Your answer will always be respected.

★ ★ ★

Every great mistake has a halfway moment,
a split second when it can be recalled
and perhaps remedied.

— PEARL S. BUCK

–81–

The only difference between *fear* and *excitement* is what we label it. The two are pretty much the same physiological/emotional reaction. With fear, we put a negative spin on it: "Oh, no!" With excitement, we give it some positive english: "Oh, boy!"

★ ★ ★

Don't be afraid to take a big step
if one is indicated.
You can't cross a chasm in two small jumps.
— DAVID LLOYD GEORGE

–82–

If you want to learn about fear, whatever it is you fear doing, that is the very next thing to do. Fear is not a wall; it's just an emotion. Move *through* the fear. Keep taking step after step toward the thing you want. It may become quite uncomfortable; then, suddenly, it will be less.

★　★　★

Everyone has talent.
What is rare is the courage
to follow the talent
to the dark place where it leads.

— ERICA JONG

–83–

Pain (any pain—emotional, physical, mental) has a message. Once we get the pain's message, and follow its advice, the pain goes away.

★ ★ ★

If I had a formula
for bypassing trouble,
I would not pass it round.
Trouble creates
a capacity to handle it.

— OLIVER WENDELL HOLMES

–84–

Just as fear is also excitement, stubbornness is also *determination*. It's simply a matter of shifting from "won't power" to "will power."

★ ★ ★

It's a funny thing about life;
if you refuse to accept
anything but the best,
you very often get it.

— SOMERSET MAUGHAM

−85−

An addiction is anything that has more power over you than you do.

★ ★ ★

When you stop drinking,
you have to deal with
this marvelous personality
that started you drinking
in the first place.

— JIMMY BRESLIN

–86–

The "old" word for addiction was temptation. "Lead us not into temptation" (Jesus); "My temptation is quiet" (Yeats); "I can resist everything except temptation" (Oscar Wilde).

★ ★ ★

Blessed is the man
that endureth temptation:
for when he is tried,
he shall receive the crown of life.

— JAMES 1:12

–87–

Once you overcome your addiction, you know you can overcome all things. The impossible becomes possible. The undoable, doable. The unmanageable, manageable. Overcoming an addiction even eases the process of releasing our addiction to life at the time of our death.

★ ★ ★

Why comes temptation,
but for man to meet
And master and make crouch
beneath his foot,
And so be pedestaled in triumph?

— ROBERT BROWNING

–88–

Death is a *friend*—a joyful, freeing process.

★ ★ ★

Death is a friend of ours;
and he that is not ready
to entertain him is not at home.
— FRANCIS BACON

–89–

Of course, one's belief about what happens *after* death falls into The Gap. There are, however, only three major beliefs about death in the entire Gap: first, life is purely biological; second, when you die, you go to heaven or hell; and third, reincarnation. If you take the time to explore your belief about what happens after death, you'll probably find it's not all that bad.

★　★　★

One of the situations in which everybody seems to fear loneliness is death. In tones drenched with pity, people say of someone, "He died alone." I have never understood this point of view. Who wants to have to die and be polite at the same time?

— QUENTIN CRISP

–90–

Suicide is always an option, of course. The option is, sometimes, what makes life bearable. Knowing we don't absolutely *have* to be here can make *being* here a little more bearable. I do not, however, recommend suicide. Sometimes it's only after a painful process is over that we can look back and see what we learned from the situation.

★ ★ ★

There are certain things
human beings are not permitted to know—
like what we're doing.

— WILLIAM BURROUGHS

–91–

The simple solution for disappointment depression: Get up and get moving. Physically move. Do. Act. Get going.

★ ★ ★

Perhaps the most valuable result of all education
is the ability to make yourself do the thing you have to do
when it ought to be done, whether you like it or not;
it is the first lesson that ought to be learned;
and however early a man's training begins,
it is probably the last lesson that he learns thoroughly.

— THOMAS HUXLEY

–92–

When people believe one thing and do another, they are inviting misery. If you give yourself the name, play the game. When you believe something you don't follow with your heart, intellect, and body, it hurts. Don't do that. Live your belief, or let that belief go.

★ ★ ★

One must not lose desires.
They are mighty stimulants
to creativeness, to love, and to long life.
— ALEXANDER BOGOMOLETZ

–93–

There are no emergencies, only *emergences*.
Consider each not a problem, but a challenge.
Rise to the occasion. Emerge-and-see.

★ ★ ★

When you don't have any money,
the problem is food.
When you have money, it's sex.
When you have both, it's health.
If everything is simply jake,
then you're frightened of death.

— J. P. DONLEAVY

–94–

What is your purpose? A purpose is something you discover. It's already there. It's always been there. You've lived your life by it—perhaps without fully realizing it. It's your bellwether, your personal inner divining. It tells you, in any given moment, whether you're living your life "on purpose" or not.

★ ★ ★

My function in life was to render clear what was already blindingly conspicuous.

— QUENTIN CRISP

–95–

The house, car, better body, career, or money you want—yes, even a romantic relationship, religion, or spiritual path—is simply a *method* or *behavior* to get something else, something inner, something experiential (security, fun, energy, satisfaction, love, knowledge of God, inner peace).

★ ★ ★

You must first be who you really are,
then do what you need to do,
in order to have what you want.

— MARGARET YOUNG

–96–

You can have *any*thing you want but you can't have *every*thing you want.

★ ★ ★

The greatest pleasure in life
is doing what people say
you cannot do.

— WALTER BAGEHOT

–97–

The history books are full of people who said, "I don't care if everybody thinks it's impossible, I think it's possible, I want it, and I'm going to get it (or do it)." And they did.

★ ★ ★

I just want to do God's will.
And He's allowed me to go to the mountain.
And I've looked over,
and I've seen the promised land.
So I'm happy tonight.
I'm not worried about anything.
I'm not fearing any man.

— MARTIN LUTHER KING, JR.
APRIL 3, 1968

–98–

The phrase "spending time" is a precise and accurate one. We all have only so much time this time around. Spend it well.

★ ★ ★

Who begins too much
accomplishes little.
— GERMAN PROVERB

–99–

In order to *get* what you want, it's very helpful to *know* what you want. If you don't know where you want to go, you probably won't get there.

★ ★ ★

Pick battles
big enough to matter,
small enough to win.

— JONATHAN KOZOL

–100–

The key in all this is not *what* you want, but what *you* want. When asked to list the material things they want, people often get lost in glamour: what thing can I have or do that will make me *look good?*

* * *

*I'd rather have roses on my table
than diamonds on my neck.*

— EMMA GOLDMAN

–101–

Every human achievement—from the Hoover Dam to the book you hold in your hand—began as a single thought.

★ ★ ★

In the province of the mind, what one believes to be true either is true or becomes true.

— JOHN LILLY

–102–

When thought *and* action are combined, the results are powerful—among the most powerful forces on earth.

★ ★ ★

*I have found power
in the mysteries of thought.*

— EURIPIDES
438 B.C.

–103–

Successful achievement requires the use and coordination of three things—thoughts, feelings and actions. *Thoughts* spark the process, get it going. *Feelings* keep the thoughts alive, encourage more thoughts, and get the body moving. *Action* is important to accomplish the physical tasks necessary for achievement.

★ ★ ★

To change one's life:
Start immediately.
Do it flamboyantly.
No exceptions.

— WILLIAM JAMES

–104–

Be bold. Commit and act.

★ ★ ★

*The great aim of education
is not knowledge but action.*

— HERBERT SPENCER

–105–

When you're so committed to something you *know* it's going to happen, you act as though it's going to happen. That action is a powerful affirmation.

★ ★ ★

Whatever you can do,
or dream you can, begin it.
Boldness has genius,
power and magic in it.

— GOETHE

–106–

Your word is one of the most precious things you own. Do not give it lightly. Once given, do everything within your power not to break it. A broken word, like a broken cup, cannot hold very much for very long.

★ ★ ★

Never esteem anything as of advantage to you
that will make you break your word
or lose your self-respect.

— MARCUS AURELIUS ANTONINUS
121–180 A.D.

–107–

How to keep agreements? A few suggestions: Make only agreements you plan to keep. Make every agreement important. Keep the agreements you've made. Write agreements down. Communicate at once if you discover a conflict.

★ ★ ★

I phoned my dad to tell him
I had stopped smoking.
He called me a quitter.

— STEVEN PEARL

–108–

The word *discipline* comes from two very nice words: *discipulus,* meaning pupil, and *discere,* to learn. Discipline, then, is the devotion to learning.

★ ★ ★

*For the very true beginning of wisdom
is the desire of discipline;
and the care of discipline is love.*

— WISDOM OF SOLOMON 6:17

–109–

I like to think of discipline not as forcing yourself to do without (the austerity school), but as keeping your attention focused on what you *want*.

★ ★ ★

The eye sees the open heaven,
The heart is intoxicated with bliss.
— SCHILLER

–110–

Ever wonder why it's so difficult to keep negative thoughts out of your mind for any period of time? Ever berate yourself for not being able to hold a positive thought longer? There's no need for self-reproach; the odds are so stacked against us, the fact that we have *any* positive thoughts *at all* is something of a miracle.

★ ★ ★

Beaver: *Gee, there's something wrong with just about everything, isn't there Dad?*

Ward: *Just about, Beav.*

— *LEAVE IT TO BEAVER*

–111–

Life, naturally, contains negative thoughts. *No big deal.* Really. Let them drift through your mind like leaves on a patio. There's no need to resist them, hold onto them, or entertain them (I'm talking about thoughts here, not leaves).

★ ★ ★

Nobody, as long as he moves about among the chaotic currents of life, is without trouble.

— CARL JUNG

–112–

What's important is your focus. Where—in the big picture of things—are you putting your attention? If you're focused on your goal, you can have any number of positive and negative thoughts along the way. (And probably will.)

★ ★ ★

The only reason I would take up jogging is so that I could hear heavy breathing again.

— ERMA BOMBECK

–113–

Naturally, the more positive thoughts you have, the more positive you'll feel. If you want to feel happy, think about happy things. An unending stream of "happy thoughts" is not, however, necessary to reach your goal. *Motion* and *direction* are.

★ ★ ★

The last time I saw him
he was walking down Lover's Lane
holding his own hand.

— FRED ALLEN

–114–

We all "visualize." If I asked you to draw a circle, you could do it. A circle is a visual thing. You had to "envision" it. However you "saw" the circle in your imagination, that's how you'll "see" while visualizing.

★ ★ ★

See golden days,
fruitful of golden deeds,
With Joy and Love triumphing.

— JOHN MILTON
1667

–115–

What we think about, we can become.

★ ★ ★

If you think you can do a thing,
or think you can't do a thing;
you're right.

— HENRY FORD

–116–

Affirm means to make firm, solid, more real. Thoughts—not very solid—when repeated over and over, become more and more firm. They become feelings, behaviors, methods, experiences, and things.

★ ★ ★

I'd love to see Christ come back
to crush the spirit of hate
and make men put down their guns.
I'd also like just one more hit single.

— TINY TIM

–117–

Affirmations often begin with "I am . . ." "I am a happy, healthy, wealthy person." "I am joyful no matter what is happening around me." "I am loving and kind."

★ ★ ★

The words "I am . . ." are potent words;
be careful what you hitch them to.
The thing you're claiming has
a way of reaching back and claiming you.

— A. L. KITSELMAN

–118–

Affirmations work if you use them. The more you use them, the more they work. They can be used anywhere, anytime, while doing almost anything.

★ ★ ★

Affirmation of life is the spiritual act
by which man ceases to live unreflectively and
begins to devote himself to his life with reverence
in order to raise it to its true value.
To affirm life is to deepen,
to make more inward,
and to exalt the will to live.

— ALBERT SCHWEITZER

–119–

It's a good idea to end all your affirmations with ". . . this or something better, for the highest good of all concerned." The ". . . this or something better . . ." lets ten million come in when you merely asked for a million, and ". . . for the highest good of all concerned" assures that your affirmation is fulfilled in a way that's best for everyone.

★ ★ ★

A man is not idle because he is absorbed in thought. There is a visible labor and there is an invisible labor.

— VICTOR HUGO
1862

–120–

The best comparison between effectiveness and efficiency I've heard is this: Efficiency is getting the job done *right*. Effectiveness is getting the *right job done.*

★ ★ ★

It's no good running a pig farm badly
for thirty years while saying,
"Really I was meant to be a ballet dancer."
By that time, pigs will be your style.

— QUENTIN CRISP

–121–

People who excel in life—the so-called "winners" —don't do twice as much or five times as much or a hundred times as much as "average" people. Winners, it has been shown, only do a *few percentage points more* than everybody else.

★ ★ ★

Be wiser than other people,
if you can, but do not tell them so.
— LORD CHESTERFIELD

–122–

Here is the truth about making a plan: The plan itself never works. If, however, you *do* make a plan, the chances of getting what you want significantly increase.

★ ★ ★

While one person hesitates
because he feels inferior,
the other is busy making mistakes
and becoming superior.

— HENRY C. LINK

–123–

If you're not actively involved in getting what you want, you don't really want it.

★ ★ ★

Decide what you want,
decide what you are willing
to exchange for it.
Establish your priorities
and go to work.

— H. L. HUNT

–124–

One thing's for sure: you'll spend your time doing *something*. The only question is: do you want to control your time, or do you want your time to control you?

★ ★ ★

For the things we have to learn
before we can do them,
we learn by doing them.

— ARISTOTLE

–125–

Get off your buts!

★ ★ ★

You said, "but."
I've put my finger on the whole trouble.
You're a "but" man. Don't say, "but."
That little word "but" is the difference
between success and failure.
Henry Ford said, "I'm going to invent the automobile,"
and Arthur T. Flanken said, "But . . ."

— SGT. ERNIE BILKO
THE PHIL SILVERS SHOW

–126–

Do it!

$\star$ $\star$ $\star$

*Victory belongs to
the most persevering.*

— NAPOLEON

–127–

If you want to achieve more, declare your reasons unreasonable, your excuses inexcusable.

★ ★ ★

*In Endymion, I leaped headlong into the sea,
and thereby have become better acquainted with
the soundings, the quicksands, and the rocks,
than if I had stayed upon the green shore,
and piped a silly pipe, and took tea
and comfortable advice.*

— JOHN KEATS
1818

−128−

We all live within the comfort zone. It's the arena of activities we have done often enough to feel comfortable doing again.

★ ★ ★

Life is either a daring adventure or nothing.
Security does not exist in nature,
nor do the children of men
as a whole experience it.
Avoiding danger is no safer
in the long run than exposure.

— HELEN KELLER

–129–

When we do something new, something different, we push against the parameters of our comfort zone. If we do the new thing often enough, we overcome the fear, guilt, unworthiness, hurt feelings, and anger, and our comfort zone expands. If we back off and honor the limitation, our comfort zone shrinks. It's a dynamic, living thing, always expanding or contracting.

▲　▲　▲

We confide in our strength,
without boasting of it;
we respect that of others,
without fearing it.

— THOMAS JEFFERSON

–130–

Do it. Feel the fear, and do it anyway. *Physically move* to accomplish those things you choose. Learn to love it all.

★ ★ ★

A coward dies a hundred deaths,
a brave man only once . . .
But then, once is enough, isn't it?

— JUDGE HARRY STONE
NIGHT COURT

–131–

How long will it take to get what you want? How much work is enough? When you have what you want, that was enough. Until then, it wasn't.

★ ★ ★

Let us, then, be up and doing,
With a heart for any fate;
Still achieving, still pursuing,
Learn to labor and to wait.

— LONGFELLOW
1839

–132–

To use your goals and aspirations as small talk over dinner dissipates their energy. But to meet with like minds and discuss the challenges and triumphs of mastering your life— *that* has power, splendor, and esteem.

★ ★ ★

I think and think for months and years.
Ninety-nine times, the conclusion is false.
The hundredth time I am right.

— ALBERT EINSTEIN

–133–

The support you can gather from good friends, groups and your Master Teacher is formidable. The encouragement you can give them in return (yes, even Master Teachers need a little encouragement) is substantial.

★ ★ ★

*A friend is a gift
you give yourself.*
— ROBERT LOUIS STEVENSON

–134–

You are worthy of all the good that comes your way. How do I know? If you weren't worthy, it wouldn't come your way.

★ ★ ★

I am open to receive
With every breath I breathe.
— MICHAEL SUN

–135–

When you think you've had all the joy you can tolerate, you've only reached *your* limit, not joy's.

★ ★ ★

*Gladness of the heart
is the life of a man,
and the joyfulness of a man
prolongeth his days.*
— ECCLESIASTICUS 30:22

–136–

Ever watch anyone have a temper tantrum? Or go on and on about how unfairly the world treated her? Or cry over the loss of a love he didn't much like anyway? Ever watch a fit of jealousy, pettiness, or vindictiveness?

★ ★ ★

Grow up!

— JOAN RIVERS

–137–

Replacing a negative memory with a
positive one heals it.

★ ★ ★

*I don't have
a warm personal enemy left.
They've all died off.
I miss them terribly
because they helped define me.*

— CLAIRE BOOTH LUCE

–138–

Health is more than just the lack of illness—health is aliveness, energy, joy.

★ ★ ★

Health is the state
about which
medicine has nothing to say.
— W. H. AUDEN

–139–

Health is not heavy. Health is light work.

★ ★ ★

Of one thing I am certain,
the body is not
the measure of healing
—peace is the measure.

— GEORGE MELTON

–140–

Forgiving means "for giving"—
in favor of giving.

★ ★ ★

Of course God will forgive me;
that's his business.

— HEINRICH HEINE
1856

–141–

After you've forgiven the transgression and judgment, there's only one thing to do: forget them. Whatever "protection" you think you may gain from remembering past grievances is far less important than the balm of forgetting.

★ ★ ★

Education is what survives
when what has been learned
has been forgotten.

— B. F. SKINNER

–142–

Your childhood is over. Your parents did the best they could with what they knew. They gave you the greatest gift of all: Life. You don't have to *like* your parents. But it feels better if you learn to love them.

★ ★ ★

*My mother had
a great deal of trouble with me,
but I think she enjoyed it.*

— MARK TWAIN

–143–

Laugh. Out loud. Often.

★ ★ ★

Laughter is inner jogging.

— NORMAN COUSINS

–144–

Crying, like laughing, is a marvelous, natural release. People feel *so good* after a cry, I wonder why it's such a taboo.

★ ★ ★

Tears, idle tears, I know not what they mean,
Tears from the depth of some divine despair
Rise in the heart, and gather to the eyes,
In looking on the happy autumn fields,
And thinking of the days that are no more.

— ALFRED, LORD TENNYSON
1847

–145–

Wealth is health, happiness, abundance, prosperity, riches, loving, caring, sharing, learning, knowing what you want, opportunity, enjoying, and balance.

★ ★ ★

I'm an experienced woman;
I've been around . . .Well, all right,
I might not've been around,
but I've been . . . nearby.

— MARY RICHARDS
THE MARY TYLER MOORE SHOW

–146–

Unlike money, wealth is not just what you have.
Wealth is what you can do without.

★ ★ ★

To live content with small means;
to seek elegance rather than luxury,
and refinement rather than fashion;
to be worthy, not respectable, and wealthy, not rich;
to study hard, think quietly, talk gently, act frankly;
to listen to stars and birds, to babes and sages, with open heart;
to bear all cheerfully, do all bravely, await occasions, hurry never.
In a word, to let the spiritual, unbidden and unconscious,
grow up through the common. This is to be my symphony.

— WILLIAM HENRY CHANNING
1810–1884

–147–

We have so many conflicting beliefs about money in our culture. Some are uplifting, some are "downpushing." It's little wonder, that the way most people feel about money is simply *confused*.

★ ★ ★

From birth to age 18, a girl needs good parents,
from 18 to 35 she needs good looks,
from 35 to 55 she needs a good personality,
and from 55 on she needs cash.

— SOPHIE TUCKER

–148–

If you want more money, here's how to get it: reduce the number of limiting beliefs you have about money; increase the positive beliefs you hold; do what it takes to get money.

★ ★ ★

Lack of money
is the root of all evil.
— GEORGE BERNARD SHAW

–149–

Money is simply a symbol of energy. I use money so that, as an author, I don't have to carry books with me and trade them for whatever it is I want.

★ ★ ★

Many a time we've been down to our last piece of fatback.
And I'd say, "Should we eat it, or render it down for soap?"
Your Uncle Jed would say, "Render it down.
God will provide food for us poor folks,
but we gotta do our own washin'."

— GRANNY
THE BEVERLY HILLBILLIES

–150–

Learn to sacrifice. I think you'd be better off sacrificing greed, lust, hurt, judgments, demands, spoiledness, envy, jealousy, vindictiveness. You don't need them anymore.

★ ★ ★

Don't go to piano bars where
young, unemployed actors get up and sing.
Definitely don't <u>be</u> a young, unemployed actor
who gets up and sings.

— TONY LANG

–151–

The idea that life is take, take, take (learn, learn, learn) needs to be balanced with the idea that life is also giving (teaching). Receiving and giving (learning and teaching) are two parts of a single flow, like breathing in (receiving) and breathing out (giving). One cannot take place without the other.

★ ★ ★

Life is something like a trumpet.
If you don't put anything in,
you won't get anything out.

— W. C. HANDY

–152–

We seem to be students of those people who know more than we do, doers with those who know just about as much as we do, and teachers of those who know less than we do. Life is a process of doing, learning, enjoying, *and* teaching.

★ ★ ★

Honest criticism is hard to take,
particularly from a relative, a friend,
an acquaintance, or a stranger.

— FRANKLIN P. JONES

–153–

This learning-doing-teaching happens in almost every area of life—and all three often happen simultaneously. The child we are teaching to read and write is, in the same moment, teaching us innocence and wonder.

★   ★   ★

The Sea of Galilee has an outlet.
It gets to give.
It gathers in its riches that it may pour them out again
to fertilize the Jordan plain.
But the Dead Sea with the same water makes horror.
For the Dead Sea has no outlet. It gets to keep.

— HARRY EMERSON FOSDICK

–154–

When the server is ready, the service appears.

★ ★ ★

Boy: *Teach me what you know, Jim.*

Reverend Jim: *That would take hours, Terry. Ah, what the heck! We've all got a little Obi Wan Kenobie in us.*

— TAXI

–155–

Gratitude comes from the root word *gratus,* which means pleasing. When you are grateful, *then* you are pleased, not by the thing, but by the gratitude. In other words, in order to feel pleased, be grateful.

★ ★ ★

You are a member
of the British royal family.
We are <u>never</u> tired,
and we all <u>love</u> hospitals.

— QUEEN MARY

–156–

The attitude of gratitude: the great, full feeling.

★ ★ ★

Tomorrow is the most important thing in life.
Comes into us at midnight very clean.
It's perfect when it arrives
and it puts itself in our hands.
It hopes we've learned something
from yesterday.

— JOHN WAYNE

–157–

It takes great strength to be happy.

* * *

*Happiness is having
a large, loving, caring,
close-knit family
in another city.*

— GEORGE BURNS

–158–

Happiness requires courage, stamina, persistence, fortitude, perseverance, bravery, boldness, valor, vigor, concentration, solidity, substance, backbone, grit, guts, moxie, nerve, pluck, resilience, spunk, tenacity, tolerance, will power, chutzpah, and a good thesaurus.

★ ★ ★

I hate quotations.

— EMERSON

–159–

If you think happiness is easy, think again. The *theory* of happiness is simple; so simple, in fact, it can be stated in a parenthesis ("to be happy, think happy thoughts") in the middle of a not-very-long sentence. The successful *implementation* of that theory—that's where the courage, stamina, etc., come in.

★ ★ ★

Rule #1: *Don't sweat the small stuff.*

Rule #2: *It's all small stuff.*

— DR. MICHAEL MANTELL

–160–

You don't *have* to do anything.

★ ★ ★

*If you don't like
what you're doing,
you can always
pick up your needle
and move to another groove.*
— TIMOTHY LEARY

–161–

Hurry up and be patient! The sooner you're patient, the easier your life will become. Really. When you're patient, you can relax and enjoy the ride. So, quickly, hurry up and be patient!

★ ★ ★

Patience creates confidence, decisiveness
and a rational outlook,
which eventually leads to success.

— BRIAN ADAMS

–162–

Live now.

★ ★ ★

We are here and it is now.
Further than that,
all knowledge
is moonshine.

— H. L. MENCKEN

–163–

There is nothing you need to do to become worthy. You already *are* worthy. You don't even have to discover your worthiness. You can feel utterly worthless and still be worthy.

★   ★   ★

She knows what is
the best purpose of education:
not to be frightened by the best
but to treat it as part of daily life.

— JOHN MASON BROWN

–164–

If you want to think better about yourself and feel better about yourself, learn to improve your self-esteem.

★ ★ ★

So much is a man worth
as he esteems himself.
— FRANÇOIS RABELAIS
1532

–165–

Increasing your self-esteem is easy. You simply do good things, *and remember that you did them.*

★ ★ ★

Ofttimes nothing profits more
Than self-esteem,
grounded on just and right
Well managed.

— JOHN MILTON
1667

–166–

Make a list of all the good things you do. Then review the list. Often.

★ ★ ★

Life consists not
in holding good cards
but in playing
those you hold well.

— JOSH BILLINGS

–167–

You might like to try any number of meditative and contemplative techniques available—or you might just want to sit quietly and relax.

★   ★   ★

*This art of resting the mind
and the power of dismissing from it
all care and worry is probably
one of the secrets of energy
in our great men.*

— CAPTAIN J. A. HADFIELD

–168–

Some people think meditation takes time *away* from physical accomplishment. Taken to extremes, of course, that's true. Most people, however, find that meditation *creates* more time than it *takes*.

★ ★ ★

Your vision will become clear
only when you can look into your own heart.
Who looks outside, dreams;
who looks inside, awakes.

— CARL JUNG

–169–

One insight gleaned during a few minutes of meditation might save *hours,* perhaps *days* of unnecessary work. That's what we mean when we say—from a purely practical point of view—meditation can make more time than it takes.

★ ★ ★

Men stumble over the truth from time to time,
but most pick themselves up and hurry off
as if nothing happened.

— SIR WINSTON CHURCHILL

–170–

If you want peace, stop fighting with your thoughts. When you're not against yourself or others, you are at peace. Peace.

★ ★ ★

First keep the peace within yourself,
then you can also bring peace to others.

— THOMAS à KEMPIS
1420

–171–

How does one find and maintain balance? Vigilance. Internal vigilance. Internal vigilance is the price of freedom.

★　★　★

Fortunate, indeed, is the man
who takes exactly the right measure of himself,
and holds a just balance between
what he can acquire and what he can use,
be it great or be it small!

— PETER LATHAM
1789–1875

–172–

You are a Master. You might as well get good at it.

* * *

His word burned like a lamp.

— ECCLESIASTICUS 48:1

–173–

Loving is an action. *Love* is a feeling. The difference between love and loving, is the difference between fish and fishing. I like *loving*—the moving, growing, changing, active, dynamic interplay (inner play?) between self and others, and between self and self.

★   ★   ★

Joe, never feel guilty about
having warm human feelings
toward anyone.

— BEN CARTWRIGHT
BONANZA

–174–

Our loving is a work in progress. We are continuously refining it, honing it, adding to it, shaping it. This is what we *think* we are doing. We also know love is continuously refining, honing, adding to, and shaping *us*.

★ ★ ★

People think love is an emotion.
Love is good sense.

— KEN KESEY

–175–

Loving starts with the individual. When we want loving from someone else to "make us whole," we know we are not giving ourselves the loving we need.

★ ★ ★

The very purpose of existence
is to reconcile the glowing opinion
we hold of ourselves with
the appalling things that other people
think about us.

— QUENTIN CRISP

–176–

When we give ourselves the loving we need (and it takes so little time when we actually *do* it!), our time with others tends to be joyful, graceful, playful, touching—in each moment complete.

★　★　★

Man's main task in life
is to give birth to himself,
to become
what he potentially is.

— ERICH FROMM

–177–

Loving is the greatest teacher.

★ ★ ★

*We must trust the perfection
of the creation so far as to believe
that whatever curiosity the order of things
has awakened in our minds,
the order of things can satisfy.*

— EMERSON

–178–

Take good care.

School is still in session.

★ ★ ★

Fred Sanford: *Didn't you learn anything being my son? Who do you think I'm doing this all for?*

Lamont Sanford: *Yourself.*

Fred: *Yeah, you learned something.*

— *SANFORD AND SON*

–179–

Enjoy.

*For more information on our books and
unabridged audio tapes,
please write to*

*Prelude Press
8159 Santa Monica Boulevard
Los Angeles, CA 90046*

or call

1-800-LIFE-101

Thank You!

Appendix—For Further Study

Thank you for reading **The Portable LIFE 101**. If you'd like more information on any of the "lessons" in this book, here are the page numbers on which the exerpts and quotations can be found in the original **LIFE 101**.

Index